Mastering Typescript Advanced Types and Decorators

Table of Contents

Chapter 1. Introduction

In this Special Report, we delve deep into the advanced aspects of TypeScript that are critical in modern, complex web development - 'Advanced Types' and 'Decorators'. TypeScript, a statically typed superset of JavaScript, brings powerful static type-checking and object-oriented programming capabilities into the JavaScript world. This report squarely focuses on its enhanced features that are often not well-understood, yet paramount to mastering TypeScript. We elucidate intricate concepts such as conditional types, mapped types, decorator factories, and so much more, in a concise, clear, and comprehensive manner. Regardless of your experience with TypeScript, if you yearn to gain mastery over its advanced facets, this report is tailor-made for you. Let's take a momentous leap in your TypeScript proficiency together!

Chapter 2. Basics of TypeScript: A Brief Refresher

Before we explore the advanced aspects of TypeScript, it's essential to have a solid foundation in its basics. This refresher section will serve as a primer or a bridge for those familiar with JavaScript to transition smoothly into TypeScript.

TypeScript is a statically-typed, object-oriented programming language developed and maintained by Microsoft. It is a superset of JavaScript, implying that it extends JavaScript by adding types and other features. The main benefit of TypeScript is its robust static typing because it catches mistakes early through a type checker and enhances code quality and understandability.

2.1. Defining Variables

In TypeScript, you can define a variable using 'const', 'let', or 'var'.

```
let message: string = 'hello there!';
const pi: number = 3.1415;
```

In this example, the `: string` and `: number` parts tell TypeScript that `message` is a string, and `pi` is a number.

2.2. Basic Types

TypeScript supports many of the same simple types as JavaScript. Let's discuss them in detail.

- `Boolean`: The most basic datatype, represents a logical entity and can have two values: true or false.

```
let isDone: boolean = false;
```

- Number: As in JavaScript, all numbers in TypeScript are stored as floating-point values.

```
let decimal: number = 6;
let hex: number = 0xf00d;
let binary: number = 0b1010;
let octal: number = 0o744;
```

- String: Represents sequence of characters.

```
let color: string = "blue";
color = 'red';
```

2.3. Interfaces

An interface can be used to define a type and also to implement it in the class.The following shows how to define an interface.

```
interface Person {
    firstName: string;
    lastName: string;
}
```

You can then use this interface to denote certain variables or parameters.

```
function greet(person: Person) {
    return "Hello, " + person.firstName + " " +
```

```
    person.lastName;
}

let user = {firstName: "User", lastName: "Userson"};

console.log(greet(user));
```

2.4. Classes

A class in terms of OOP is a blueprint for creating objects. A class encapsulates data for the object.

```
class Greeter {
    greeting: string;

    constructor(message: string) {
        this.greeting = message;
    }

    greet() {
        return "Hello, " + this.greeting;
    }
}

let greeter = new Greeter("world");
```

Here, Greeter is a class with three members: a property named greeting, a constructor, and a method greet().

2.5. Generics

Just like C# and Java, TypeScript also has generics. Generics allow us to define the type of a member.

```typescript
function identity<T>(arg: T): T {
    return arg;
}
```

Here, we have a generic function 'identity', which can work with different datatypes and still maintain the information about the type of arguments.

As you continue exploring TypeScript, you'll find more levels of abstraction and complexity. However, this provides a good grounding. Before we meet the 'Advanced Types' and 'Decorators', you should be comfortable with these key basic concepts. Understanding these will make the advanced features a matter of continuous learning.

Chapter 3. Diving Deep into Advanced Types

In the advanced realm of TypeScript, you'll encounter a variety of unique and expressive types which help model complex type relationships, derived types, and operations on types. Some of these types include Conditional Types, Mapped Types, Index Types, and more. This exploration into "Advanced Types" will shine light on many of TypeScript's powerful features.

Data Driven Development with Advanced Types

Advanced types not only make developing code easier but allow us to make our code more expressive, thereby making it easier to read, understand, and validate.

==='Intersection Types'

Intersection types are an interesting way to create a type that combines multiple types into one. The resulting type will have all of the properties and methods from all of the intersected types. Intersection types are defined using the & symbol.

Let's plunge into the practical implementation of intersection types with an example:

```
type Name = { name: string };
type Age = { age: number };
type Person = Name & Age;
```

The Person type defined above results in a type that includes both name and age, all thanks to the intersection types.

==='Union Types'

In addition to combining types, TypeScript also allows us to define a type that could be one of several types. Known as 'Union Types', they are denoted with the symbol |.

Let's explore an example to illustrate the usage of union types:

```
type Button = { content: string };
type Input = { value: string };
type FormElement = Button | Input;
```

This implies your `FormElement` can either be a `Button` or an `Input`. Union types are a powerful way to allow flexible typing and provide ways for your code to check and behave correctly based on the actual type used.

==='Literal Types'

Literal types in TypeScript are subtypes that take on a specific set value. Basically, a literal is a more concrete subtype of a collective type. This subset type only accepts the exact value assigned to it. We can have string literal types, numeric literal types, and Boolean literal types.

An example of literal types can be seen below:

```
type ButtonType = "submit" | "reset";
let button: ButtonType;
button = "submit"; // this is correct
button = "push"; // this will throw a TypeScript error
```

While `ButtonType` is a subtype of string, it only permits the exact values "submit" and "reset".

==='Mapped Types'

Mapped types are an advanced, powerful feature of TypeScript that enables creating new types based on transformations from old types. Essentially, mapped types allow us to apply a readonly modifier, transform property types, or add new properties.

Let's look at an example of a simple mapped type:

```
type ReadonlyPerson = {
    readonly [P in keyof Person]: Person[P];
};
```

The ReadonlyPerson type is a mapped type that takes every property in Person and transforms it into a read-only property.

==='Conditional Types'

Another feature offered by TypeScript's advanced typing system is conditional types, which select one of two possible types based on a condition expressed as a type relationship test.

Let's illustrate with an example:

```
type TypeName<T> =
    T extends string ? "string" :
    T extends number ? "number" :
    "object";
```

A conditional type TypeName<T> takes a type parameter T, and then various branches are checked. If T extends string, it returns the literal type "string". If not, it checks whether T extends number. If yes, then it returns the literal type "number". If not, it simply returns "object". Therefore, the type represented by TypeName<T> will vary, according to which branch is selected.

This expedition into TypeScript's advanced type system underscores the language's diverse and nuanced features enhancing web development's precision and readability. Advanced types show how TypeScript is not just about applying types to variables, but also using those types to transform and validate your code proactively. As we continue exploring TypeScript, new possibilities keep unfolding at every corner. Let us continue the code-filled journey and delve into other features like decorators in our next chapter.

Chapter 4. Understanding and Implementing Union and Intersection Types

Let's dive right into one of TypeScript's most intriguing features - Union and Intersection types. Union types are incredibly powerful and are frequently used for flexible APIs and handling diverse sets of data. They allow you to write code that works with values that might be of several different types.

4.1. Union Types

Union types represent a value that could be one of several distinct types. We index them using a pipe (|). For instance, the typical use case for union types is in function arguments that accept different types of input.

```
let myUnionType: string | number | boolean;
myUnionType = 'Hello world';
myUnionType = 42;
myUnionType = true;
```

In the preceding example, myUnionType is a union type variable that accepts string, number, or boolean.

Union types can significantly increase the flexibility of your code. However, they also require you to write additional type checks. If you operate on a union type, you need to make sure all possible types can handle the operation. Consider the following example.

```
function handleInput(input: string | number) {
```

```
    return input.toUpperCase();
}
```

Here the compiler would throw an error because a number does not
have a toUpperCase() method. A wise idea would be to use
TypeScript's type guards:

```
function handleInput(input: string | number) {
  if (typeof input === "string") {
    return input.toUpperCase();
  } else {
    return input;
  }
}
```

This way, you ensure that the toUpperCase() method is only called
when input is a string.

4.2. Intersection Types

Intersection types are a way of combining multiple types into one.
This is particularly useful when you want to merge various types'
capabilities together. You can think of intersection types as "and" - a
value is of an intersection type if it is of all the types in the
intersection.

We index intersection types using an ampersand (&). Below is a basic
example:

```
type Name = {
  name: string;
};
```

```typescript
type Age = {
  age: number;
};

type Person = Name & Age;

let person: Person = {
  name: "John",
  age: 30
};
```

The Person type is an intersection between Name and Age, which means
a valid Person should satisfy both Name and `Age's requirements.

Intersection can also be used to extend or mix classes:

```typescript
class X {
  methodX(): void {}
}

class Y {
  methodY(): void {}
}

type XY = X & Y;

const xy: XY = {...new X(), ...new Y()};

xy.methodX(); // OK
xy.methodY(); // OK
```

In this example, XY is a type, which is the intersection of X and Y.
Hence, an object of type XY can access both `X's and `Y's methods.

Now, you must understand that intersection types are not as

frequently used as union types. This can be attributed to JavaScript's nature, which is more inclining towards the unionized systems of handling elements. Being a superset of JavaScript, TypeScript also tends to lean in that direction.

4.3. Nuances in Using Union and Intersection Types

While working with union and intersection types, one must be wary of potential pitfalls. The most notable one being that when forming unions of overlapping type's methods, TypeScript takes a rather conservative approach – methods present in only some members of the union are declared as optional.

Delving into advanced TypeScript, the discovery of union and intersection types may seem like uncharted territory. But their mastery is the threshold to dynamic web application development via TypeScript. It's like an artist experimenting with varied hues for that perfect palette or a musician exploring the myriad pitches to hit the perfect note. Seek comfort in the discomfort of learning these new constructs, and rest assured, the mastery of TypeScript is not far.

Remember - 'Intermediate layers merely shape union types, intersections define them.'

We hope this deep dive into union and intersection types provides the clarity and understanding you need to effectively utilize these TypeScript features. Dive in, explore, learn, modify, implement, and create powerful, flexible, and maintainable TypeScript applications. Happy coding!

Chapter 5. Exploring Generic Types and Constraints

In TypeScript, Generic Types, as the name suggests, provide a way to make components work with any data type and not restrict to one data type. Generic types are among the most powerful features of TypeScript, allowing you to define standard functions, classes, or interfaces that can work with a variety of types while maintaining type safety. Further enhancing this power, TypeScript also allows applying constraints over these generic types. Let's begin our exploration of these two concepts.

5.1. Understanding Generic Types

Let's begin our journey by understanding the idea behind Generic Types. These types allow you to write reusable components that can work over several types rather than a single one. This functionality promotes code reusability and maintainability.

To grasp the idea, consider a simple function to return an array's first element:

```
function getFirstElement(arr: any[]): any {
  return arr[0];
}
```

Here, the `getFirstElement` function will accept any array, be it numbers, strings, objects, and return the first element. While this grants some flexibility, we lose some important type information. For instance, if we pass an array of numbers, we would expect a number in return, not just any type.

To resolve this issue, TypeScript provides us with 'Generic Types'.

Check out the updated version of the function below:

```
function getFirstElement<T>(arr: T[]): T {
  return arr[0];
}
```

In the function `getFirstElement<T>(arr: T[]): T`, "T" is a placeholder for any type that will be determined at the function invocation. By implementing it this way, we are not losing the array type information when returning. This helps when a type-specific operation is performed on the returned element.

5.2. Constraints in Generic Types

Constraints in TypeScript are a way to control the properties and methods that a Generic Type might have. When we define a Generic Type, it represents a broad spectrum of types. However, we may need to restrict this spectrum in context to a specific implementation.

Look at the following function as an example:

```
function getLength<T>(item: T): number {
  return item.length;
}
```

This function `getLength<T>(item: T): number` tries to return the length of the given item. The function would work fine for an array or a string, but what if we pass a number or any other type that lacks a `length` property? It would result in an error.

To prevent this situation, TypeScript allows us to define constraint on 'T'. Here's how to do it:

```
function getLength<T extends { length: number }>(item:
T): number {
  return item.length;
}
```

In the function `getLength<T extends { length: number }>(item: T): number`, we added `{ length: number }` as a constraint on 'T'. This code imposes that 'T' should have a property 'length' that is a number.

5.3. Using Multiple Type Variables

We can use more than one type variable. This capability allows us to write functions that can work with multiple unknown types in a type-safe manner.

Consider the following example:

```
function combine<T, U>(first: T, second: U): [T, U] {
  return [first, second];
}
```

In this function `combine<T, U>(first: T, second: U): [T, U]`, we've used two type variables, 'T' and 'U'. This allows us to handle two values that can be of any type and return a tuple with these two values, all while keeping the type information intact.

5.4. Default Type Arguments

TypeScript allows us to have default types that the type variable will be set to if no type is provided while invoking the function.

Consider the following function:

```typescript
function greetText<T = string>(text: T) {
  console.log("Greet Text:", text);
}
```

Here we specify T = string which declares 'T' as type 'string' by default. We can still invoke the function with another type, but if no type is provided, the function will work with type 'string'.

Generics and Constraints in TypeScript make it incredibly powerful while keeping type safety intact. They deliver the perfect balance of flexibility, by working with multiple data types, and stability, by helping maintain type safety throughout. As we have seen, they allow us to write code that is reusable, maintainable, and understandable. They are indeed a significant component in the armament of any TypeScript developer.

Chapter 6. Mastering Conditional Types

Understanding conditional types, with their ability to conditionally select types based on certain conditions, has the potential to profoundly impact how we approach type manipulations in TypeScript. These offer the power to express non-uniform type mappings, a capability that's beyond creating direct, same-for-all fields mappings.

6.1. The Basic Idea of Conditional Types

Let's begin with an understanding of the core idea of conditional types. In simple terms, TypeScript conditional types allow you to choose the type for a generic variable based on a condition. That is, we provide TypeScript with some type of check, and TypeScript then gives us one type if that check is true and another type if the check is false.

The basic syntax for defining a conditional type is as follows:

```
[code]
T extends U ? X : Y
[/code]
```

Here, T is the tested type. If it can be assigned to U(i.e., if T extends U), X type would be selected, otherwise, Y type is chosen. Keep in mind that this is not a runtime condition but a static type check performed by the TypeScript's type system.

6.2. Conditional Types and Control Flow Analysis

One of the vital underpinnings of conditional types is TypeScript's control flow analysis. Without it, conditional types wouldn't be possible or at least not feasible in a statically typed language like TypeScript.

Control flow analysis allows TypeScript to analyze your code and deduce the types of variables at any position, which in turn facilitates handling type variations. It is the operative mechanism that aids TypeScript in determining whether `T extends U` and then choosing between `X` and `Y`.

Just like with runtime control flow where the flow of execution could diverge, here too, as we follow the type flow, there can be divergences — and these divergences are what we capture with conditional types.

6.3. Practical Uses of Conditional Types

Let's examine a few practical examples to illuminate the real-world uses of conditional Typing.

Consider a scenario where we desire to wrap all properties of a type into a promise. This might be a situation where we have an asynchronous API which returns a type, and we want to have a similar type but with every property being a promise.

For this, consider a type `Person`: [code] type Person = { name: string; age: number; } [/code]

If we want to create a new type `PersonAsync` where each property is a

Promise, we would use conditional types.

```
[code]
type WrapPromise<T> = {
  [P in keyof T]: Promise<T[P]>;
}


type PersonAsync = WrapPromise<Person>;
[/code]
```

Our WrapPromise is a mapped type that maps over all keys (properties) in an inputted type T, and returns a Promise of the original property type.

6.4. Advanced Conditionals: Distributive Conditional Types

A crucial aspect to understanding conditional types is the concept of distributivity. In the context of TypeScript, a distributive conditional type is applied to the union of types, selectively acting on each member. Let's examine this with the following type:

```
[code]
type Conditional<T> = T extends string ? string[] :
number[];
[/code]
```

Observing this type, you might expect that applying Conditional to a union type like string | number would result in (string[] | number[]). However, TypeScript distributively applies the conditional type to each member of the union:

```
[code]
type Result = Conditional<string | number>;  // Result
is string[] | number[]
[/code]
```

This distributive property opens up a vast avenue of possibilities and can be judiciously leveraged to model complex behaviors at compile time.

6.5. Conditional Types With Infer

Another advanced facet of conditional types is the infer keyword, which allows us to infer a type within other types.

Should you wish to create a type that extracts the return type of a function, you would make use of infer in a conditional type. Here's how to do it:

```
[code]
type ReturnType<T> = T extends (...args: any[]) => infer
R ? R : never;
[/code]
```

Initially, we are checking if T extends a function. If it does, we employ infer to extract the return type and assign it to R. If the condition fails, we default to never. This way we can fetch the return type of any function.

As you delve deeper into TypeScript, you will recognize the utility of the infer keyword within conditional and other advanced types to undertake intricate type operations with ease.

Heretofore we've been through a lot: the core idea, practical uses, advanced control flow, distributivity, and the `infer` keyword. Your dexterity with these concepts determines how you work with TypeScript at an industry level, especially when dealing with large-scale or complex applications. RelayCommand and keep experimenting with conditional types for a nuanced understanding of their potential.

Chapter 7. The Magic of Mapped Types

Mapped types are an advanced feature of TypeScript, enabling us to create new types based on existing types. The basic idea behind mapped types is to transform a given type into a new type, potentially adding, modifying, or removing certain properties or methods.

7.1. The Basics of Mapped Types

When considering TypeScript's mapped types, we have to start with their basic structure. Mapped types are characterised by the `in` keyword, which iterates over the keys of a type and applies a certain structure to them.

The following is the basic structure of a mapped type:

```
type MappedType<Type> = {
    [Properties in keyof Type]: SomeType;
};
```

The `keyof` keyword in TypeScript produces a union of literal types from the keys of an object type, i.e. it is able to extract all keys from a given type `Type` in this case.

To understand mapped types, consider this simple example:

```
type OriginalType = {
    prop1: string;
    prop2: number;
};
```

```
type MappedType = {
    [P in keyof OriginalType]: boolean;
};

let example: MappedType = {
    prop1: false,
    prop2: true,
};

console.log(example); // Output: { prop1: false, prop2:
true }
```

Here, we have defined an OriginalType with prop1 and prop2. We then create a new type MappedType which iterates over all keys in OriginalType and maps each property to boolean. Consequently, an object of MappedType must have prop1 and prop2, but both of these properties must be boolean.

7.2. Utilising the Readonly Modifier

mapped types offer us a great way to create variations of types. Consider the Readonly modifier which is predefined within TypeScript's library. The Readonly<Type> mapped type signifies that all properties of Type are readonly.

```
type OriginalType = {
    prop1: string;
    prop2: number;
};

type ReadonlyOriginalType= Readonly<OriginalType>;

let example: ReadonlyOriginalType= {
```

```
    prop1: 'hello',
    prop2: 42,
};


// Trying to modify prop1 will raise a compile error.
example.prop1 = 'world'; // Error: property prop1 is
read-only.
```

Readonly<OriginalType> creates a new type where all the properties of
OriginalType are readonly. The object example of type
ReadonlyOriginalType cannot be modified once it's defined.

7.3. Modifying Optional Properties

Consider the Partial modifier in TypeScript which allows us to mark
all properties of a type as optional.

```
type OriginalType = {
    prop1: string;
    prop2: number;
};

type PartialOriginalType = Partial<OriginalType>;

let example1: PartialOriginalType = {
    prop1: 'hello',
};

let example2: PartialOriginalType = {
    prop2: 42,
};

console.log(example1); // Output: { prop1: 'hello' }
console.log(example2); // Output: { prop2: 42 }
```

Here, `Partial<OriginalType>` creates a new type that can have `prop1` and `prop2`. However, it is not necessary to have either of these properties within any `PartialOriginalType` object.

7.4. Extracting Property Names

We can extract property names with certain characteristics from a type. Consider the following `ExtractStringKeys` mapped type that extracts keys of string properties from a type:

```
type OriginalType = {
    prop1: string;
    prop2: number;
    prop3: boolean;
};

type StringKeys = {
    [K in keyof OriginalType]: OriginalType[K] extends
string ? K : never
}[keyof OriginalType];

type StringPropType = Pick<OriginalType, StringKeys>;
```

Here, we are creating a new type `StringKeys` that sifts through all keys of `OriginalType` and retains only those keys whose corresponding properties in `OriginalType` are string.

In the end, we create a new type `StringPropType` using `Pick` utility type that selects `prop1` from `OriginalType`, as it is the only key marked by `StringKeys`.

In conclusion, mapped types offer a compelling mechanism to adapt existing types without duplicating or invasive modifications. This can make your TypeScript codebase more robust, flexible, and maintainable. Whether you are just starting in TypeScript or have been using it for some time, exploring and utilising mapped types will certainly be beneficial.

Chapter 8. Introduction to TypeScript Decorators

To address the advanced facet of TypeScript crucial to complex web development applications - TypeScript Decorators, we commence this exploration at the absolute beginning. A foundational understanding of this feature will arm us with the capabilities to unfold the more advanced features and functionality it provides.

Decorators, introduced in TypeScript version 1.5, are a special kind of declaration that can be attached to a class declaration, method, property, or parameter. Underneath, Decorators use the form '@expression', where 'expression' is a function that gets called at runtime with information about the decorated declaration.

Decorators are proposed for a future version of JavaScript, and TypeScript's decorators act as a way to experiment with this proposition, enabling us to use them in our TypeScript code.

8.1. Unwrapping Decorators

To start with, imagine decorators as wrappers. When you wrap a gift, the wrapping paper and the ribbon you choose add aesthetics and some level of abstraction to the gift inside. Similarly, decorators wrap around TypeScript classes or members and add annotations or modify their behaviors.

At a fundamental level, a decorator is just a function. Decorators in TypeScript are not a new concept; they are known as annotations in AtScript, which is a superset of TypeScript.

To give you an example, have a look at the following TypeScript class:

```
class Car {
```

```
    constructor(public model: string) {}
  }
```

If we were to add a decorator to it, we might end up with something
like this:

```
@log
class Car {
    constructor(public model: string) {}
  }
```

Here, *@log* is a decorator. It's succinct, clean, adds meaningful
semantics to the class, and doesn't clutter up the core logic of the
class. This feature allows us to write cleaner, more manageable, and
modular code.

8.2. Base Forms of Decorators

In TypeScript, decorators can be applied in four different contexts or
have four base forms.

1. Class Decorators

2. Method Decorators

3. Property Decorators

4. Parameter Decorators

Let's take an in-depth look at each base form of decorator.

8.3. Class Decorators

A Class Decorator is declared just before a class declaration. The class
decorator applies to the constructor of the class and can be used to

observe, modify or replace a class definition. A class decorator cannot be used in a declaration file, on a declare class, or in any other ambient context.

The expression for the class decorator will be called as a function at runtime, with the constructor of the decorated class as its only argument.

For instance, if we declare a *@sealed* decorator as follows:

```
function sealed(constructor: Function) {
  Object.seal(constructor);
  Object.seal(constructor.prototype);
}
```

We can then use it to seal up our *Car* class like so:

```
@sealed
class Car {
  constructor(public model: string) {}
}
```

In the aforementioned code, we've sealed both the constructor function and its prototype, stopping other parts of the code from changing it, e.g., by adding methods.

8.4. Method Decorators

A Method Decorator is declared just before a method declaration. The method decorator can be used to observe, modify, or replace a method definition. A method decorator cannot be used in a declaration file, on an overload, or in any other ambient context.

The expression for the method decorator will be called as a function at runtime, with the following three arguments:

1. Either the constructor function of the class for a static member, or the prototype of the class for an instance member.

2. The member's name.

3. The Property Descriptor for the member.

For instance, consider the following *@enumerable* decorator:

```
function enumerable(value: boolean) {
  return function (
    target: any,
    propertyKey: string,
    descriptor: PropertyDescriptor
  ) {
    descriptor.enumerable = value;
  };
}
```

We can use the above *@enumerable* decorator to make a method in our *Car* class non-enumerable:

```
class Car {
  constructor(public model: string) {}

  @enumerable(false)
  start() {
    // method implementation
  }
}
```

With this, the *start* function on the *Car* class is not enumerable anymore.

8.5. Property Decorators

A Property Decorator is declared with the name of the property to act upon. Unlike a Method Decorator, it does not contain a Property Descriptor as it can't modify the result, instead, it merely observes the property it is decorating.

The decorator will be called as a function at runtime, where it will receive the following two arguments:

1. Either the constructor function of the class for a static member, or the prototype of the class for an instance member.

2. The name of the member.

If we were to set up a *@format* decorator to change the way our *Car's* model number is displayed, we might write it like this:

```
function format(target: any, propertyKey: string) {
  let _val = target[propertyKey];
  const getter = function () {
    return "Car Model -> " + _val;
  };
  const setter = function (newVal) {
    _val = newVal;
  };
  if (delete target[propertyKey]) {
    Object.defineProperty(target, propertyKey, {
      get: getter,
      set: setter,
      enumerable: true,
      configurable: true,
    });
  }
}
```

Our *Car* class looks like this now:

```
class Car {
  @format
  public model: string;

  constructor(model: string) {
    this.model = model;
  }
}
```

8.6. Parameter Decorators

A Parameter Decorator is declared on the parameters of a method, or
its constructor. It can be used to observe the usage of the other three
decorators within a class.

The parameter decorator will be called as a function at runtime
where it will receive the following three arguments:

1. Either the constructor function of the class for a static member,
    or the prototype of the class for an instance member.

2. The name of the member.

3. The ordinal index of the parameter in the function's parameter
    list.

For instance, a simple *@required* decorator could be written as:

```
function required(target: any, propertyKey: string,
parameterIndex: number) {
  let existingRequiredParameters: number[] =
Reflect.getOwnMetadata(
    "required",
```

```
    target,
    propertyKey
  ) || [];
  existingRequiredParameters.push(parameterIndex);
  Reflect.defineMetadata("required",
existingRequiredParameters, target, propertyKey);
}
```

And be used in the *Car* class as follows:

```
class Car {
  constructor(public model: string) {}

  drive(@required speed: number) {
    // method implementation
  }
}
```

In here, we require a speed parameter while invoking the *drive* method.

Decorators not only bring the ability to observe, manage, and modify classes, methods, properties, and parameters but also add efficiency to the development cycle by enabling better modularity and cleaner code. TypeScript's implementation of decorators bridges a gap in object-oriented JavaScript, bringing a level of sophistication and ease to your codebase without the need to resort to clunky, cluttered, and awkward workarounds.

Our subsequent discussions will revolve around the practical applications of Decorators in the real world, exploring various use-cases with hands-on examples. By the end of it, you will find yourself equipped with a robust understanding and practical knowledge of TypeScript's Decorators that will put you a step ahead of your peers in the world of modern, complex web development!

Chapter 9. Creating and Using Class Decorators

Decorators - a compelling addition to TypeScript - enhance the readability and maintainability of the code. They can be classified predominantly as class decorators, method decorators, property decorators, and parameter decorators. In this chapter, we are going to focus specifically on creating and using class decorators.

9.1. Understanding Class Decorators

Before diving into the details, let's comprehend what class decorators are. A class decorator is a special kind of declaration that is applied to a class constructor. They allow developers to observe, modify, or replace the class definition. When a class decorator is invoked, it gets the constructor of the decorated class as its argument.

To write a class decorator, simply declare a function with one argument. This argument refers to the constructor function of the class being decorated.

```
function classDecorator(target: Function) {
    // Do something with 'target'...
}
```

Here `target` is the constructor function of the class being decorated. This gives us full access to the class - its properties, methods, and metadata.

To apply this decorator, we write "@" followed by the decorator's name, just before the class definition:

```
@classDecorator
class MyClassName {
    // Class goes here...
}
```

But alone, a decorator like this doesn't do much. To unleash its full power, a class decorator needs to return something. Depending on the return type, a class decorator can behave in two different ways:

1. If the class decorator returns nothing, it can only be used to observe the class. It receives the class constructor as its sole argument, allowing it to inspect the class in various ways. But as it doesn't return anything, it can't make any modifications.

2. But, if a class decorator returns a new constructor function, it can replace the class with a new one. This makes it possible to control the behavior of the class, its instances, and to add new methods or properties.

9.2. Creating Simple Class Decorators

Let's create a basic class decorator which simply logs the name of the class.

```
function logClassName(target: Function) {
    console.log(`Class name: ${target.name}`);
}

@logClassName
class Hero {
    constructor(public name: string, public alignment:
string) { }
```

```
}
```

When you create a new instance of the class Hero, you should see "Class name: Hero" in your console log.

But let's explore a more advanced scenario where we want our class decorator to replace the whole class.

9.3. Replacing Classes with Class Decorators

To replace a class, a decorator needs to return a new constructor function. This function technically becomes a new class replacing the decorated one.

```
function sealed(constructor: Function) {
    Object.seal(constructor);
    Object.seal(constructor.prototype);
}

@sealed
class Bug {
    constructor(public name: string) { }
}
```

In the above example, the decorator sealed is sealing both the constructor function and its prototype. This means that you cannot change the structure of the class afterwards - no new methods or properties can be added.

9.4. Decorators with Arguments or Decorator Factories

There might be situations where you want your decorator to take additional parameters. This might seem impossible at first, given that TypeScript uses the decorator function to pass in the class constructor. However, there is a workaround for this issue called decorator factories.

A decorator factory is a function that returns the decorator function. Let's see this in an example:

```
function logClassWithArgs(verbose: boolean): any {
    if (verbose) {
        return (constructor: Function) =>
console.log(`Class name: ${constructor.name}`);
    } else {
        return (constructor: Function) => {  };
    }
}


@logClassWithArgs(true)
class Villain {
    constructor(public name: string, public evilPlan:
string) { }
}
```

In this example, we've altered the `logClassName` decorator to take an argument.

When you apply this to the `Villain` class with the boolean `true`, you should see "Class name: Villain" in your console. If you replace `true` with `false`, nothing will be logged.

The ability to pass in parameters to our decorators gives us vastly more control over their behavior.

In this chapter, we have delved into class decorators, learning about their purpose, creating simple decorators, replacing classes, and finally creating decorators with arguments or decorator factories. Understanding and utilizing class decorators is crucial for any TypeScript developer who wants to write succinct and maintainable code. Developing proficiency in decorators will serve you greatly when tackling larger, more complex TypeScript projects.

Chapter 10. Effectively Implementing Method and Property Decorators

To understand the effective implementation of method and property decorators, we need to be familiar with the fundamentals decorators. In TypeScript, decorators are a design pattern that allow behavior to be added to an individual object, statically or dynamically, without affecting the behavior of other objects from the same class. Properties and methods can be decorated, and once we grasp the syntax and how they work, their utility in advanced TypeScript development becomes evident.

10.1. Setting The Scene: Decorators and TypeScript

Decorators are a proposed feature for JavaScript that's already deployable in TypeScript. They provide a means to add annotations and a meta-programming syntax for class declarations and members. Decorators use the form `@expression`, where `expression` must evaluate to a function that will be called at runtime with information about the decorated declaration.

There are four places where decorators can be used:

- Classes

- Methods

- Accessors

- Properties

In this chapter, we will focus primarily on method and property decorators.

10.2. Understanding Decorators: Definitions

To properly understand how to implement method and property decorators, we have to understand what they mean in a TypeScript context:

- **Property Decorators**: They are applied to the property descriptors for class properties and static properties, and can be used to monitor, modify, or replace a property's definition.

- **Method Decorators**: These are applied to the Property Descriptor for the method, and can be used to observe, modify, or replace a method definition.

The decorating function always takes the target (prototype of the instance), the key (property name), and the property descriptor as parameters, allowing manipulation on nearly all aspects of the method or property.

10.3. Property Decorators: Implementation

Let us begin with a simple example of a property decorator:

```typescript
function simpleProperty(target: any, propertyKey:
string) {
    console.log(`Property Decorator called on:
${propertyKey}.`);
}


class PropertyDecoratorExample {
```

```
    @simpleProperty
    name: string;
}
```

In this scenario, when the `name` property is called, our decorator function `simpleProperty` is invoked, logging the fact that 'name' was accessed.

10.4. Method Decorators: Implementation

Let's start with a rudimentary example of a method decorator:

```
function simpleMethod(target: any, propertyKey: string,
descriptor: PropertyDescriptor) {
    console.log(`Method Decorator called on:
${propertyKey}.`);
}

class MethodDecoratorExample {
    @simpleMethod
    sayHello() {
        return "Hello!";
    }
}
```

When the `sayHello()` method is activated, our decorator function `simpleMethod` is called, demonstrating that the method was used.

10.5. Intermediate Decorators

As we move to more complex implementations of decorators, we start to engage problems beyond the simple logging of access. The following examples provide more concrete insight into what can be achieved:

Property Decorator to validate input:

```typescript
function ValidateInput(target: any, propertyKey: string)
{
   let _val = this[propertyKey];
   let getter = function () {
      return _val;
   };
   let setter = function (newVal) {
      if (!newVal) {
         console.error(`Invalid value: ${newVal}`);
      }
      _val = newVal;
   };
   if (delete this[propertyKey]) {
      Object.defineProperty(target, propertyKey, {
         get: getter,
         set: setter,
         enumerable: true,
         configurable: true
      });
   }
}

class InputValidator {
   @ValidateInput
   someInput: string;
}
```

In the above example, the property decorator ensures that the someInput is not assigned an empty or invalid value, overriding the setter to validate the assignment operation.

Method Decorators to Modify Return Value:

```typescript
function ModifyResult(target: any, propertyKey: string,
descriptor: PropertyDescriptor) {
    const originalMethod = descriptor.value;
    descriptor.value = function(...args: any[]) {
        const result = originalMethod.apply(this, args);
        return "Modified " + result;
    }
    return descriptor;
}

class ResultModifier {
    @ModifyResult
    sayHello() {
        return "Hello!";
    }
}
```

In the above instance, the method decorator transforms the output of `sayHello()` method and prepends `"Modified "` to it.

10.6. Tailoring Complex Decorators

In practice, decorators are rarely one-size-fits-all. Each decorator is often coded to a particular situation, with custom hooks and methods to provide the precisely tailored functionality suited to our needs. By building complex decorators that encapsulate cross-cutting concerns in an elegant way, you can significantly boost your productivity in TypeScript-based projects.

A word of advice: while decorators enable you to write cleaner and more maintainable code, they have a tangible learning curve and require a strong conceptual foundation to be truly handy. If you understand them well and use them appropriately, they can be a powerful tool in your TypeScript arsenal. However, overuse or misuse can actually decrease the maintainability of code due to increased complexity. It is important to strike a balanced approach. A decorator is just a tool - the architecture, design, and business logic still take precedence.

To conclude, decorators open up a world of possibilities for enhanced code detail and better deliverability. With method and property decorators, TypeScript allows us to perform checks, validations, modifications, and provide a raft of new functionality, all during the runtime. Though using decorators, we can maintain loosely coupled and highly scalable applications, making it easier for us to rationalize and debug as our application grows in complexity.

Chapter 11. Challenges and Solutions: Advanced TypeScript Use Cases

Let's begin by discussing some common challenges you might encounter when using advanced types in TypeScript, and how to best solve them.

11.1. Challenge: Leveraging Conditional Types

A common challenge developers face when working with TypeScript is making the most out of its available conditional types. Conditional types can help you discriminate union types, infer types and perform advanced operations in a concise way, but using them properly can be tricky.

---- Solution ----

To utilize conditional types effectively, you first need to understand how they work. In TypeScript, conditional types take a form that is similar to conditional (ternary) expressions: A extends B ? C : D.

Here, "A extends B" works as the condition. If it's true, the type will be C. If false, the type will be D.

Consider the following example:

```
type NonNullable<T> = T extends null | undefined ? never
: T;
```

"NonNullable" is a utility type that takes any type T and strips it of null and undefined. The conditional type here checks whether T can be null or undefined. If it can, it uses the special "never" type. If not, it just uses T. Using conditional types, you can create powerful and flexible utilities.

11.2. Challenge: Utilizing Mapped Types

Mapped types, another advanced feature that TypeScript provides, allows developers to create new types based on existing ones. However, it's not uncommon for developers to struggle with the right usage.

---- Solution ----

The solution to this issue lies in understanding that mapped types can help you create variants of existing types, transforming properties as required.

Consider the following example:

```
type Readonly<T> = {
    readonly [P in keyof T]: T[P];
};
```

The above example defines a mapped type "Readonly" that takes a type T and produces a new type that is the same as T, but with all its properties set as readonly. Understanding mapped types can significantly increase TypeScript's power in your hands.

11.3. Challenge: Mixed Use of Decorators

Decorators provide a way to add both annotations and a metadata programming element to class and property definitions. However, the mixed use of decorators often leads to a lot of confusion and is considered a challenge.

---- Solution ----

When you're looking to use decorators, it's crucial to remember that decorators apply functions to your classes, properties, methods, and accessors.

Consider the decorator "@sealed", which may prevent a class from being extended:

```
function sealed(constructor: Function) {
    Object.seal(constructor);
    Object.seal(constructor.prototype);
}

@sealed
class Greeter {
    greeting: string;
    constructor(message: string) {
        this.greeting = message;
    }
    greet() {
        return "Hello, " + this.greeting;
    }
}
```

In this code, the @sealed decorator is a function that seals the class constructor and its prototype, preventing new properties from being added and keeping existing ones from being removed or configured.

11.4. Challenge: Creating and Applying Decorator Factories

A common challenge with decorators is creating and applying decorator factories – functions that return a decorator.

---- Solution ----

Consider the following code snippet:

```
function color(value: string) { // this is a decorator
factory
    return function (target) { // this is the decorator
        // do something with "target" and "value"...
    }
}

@color('red')
class Apple {
}
```

In the example above, "@color('red')" is a decorator factory. When the "@color" decorator is called with a string, it returns a new decorator function. The decorator then receives the target it's applied to as its own argument.

Understanding these challenges and their solutions would provide a strong foundation for using advanced TypeScript features capably. As your proficiency with these advanced topics improves, you'll become more adept at handling complex TypeScript use cases and applications.